HAL LEONARD PIANO REPERTOIRE
Book 3 • Early Intermediate

JOURNEY THROUGH
CLASSICS

COMPILED, EDITED, AND RECORDED BY JENNIFER LINN

Dedicated in loving memory to my mother and first teacher,
Geraldine Ruth Ryan Lange.

To access recorded performances online, visit:
www.halleonard.com/mylibrary

Enter Code
5685-7257-0638-4074

Cover Art: Rose Garden, 1876 (oil on canvas) by Claude Monet (1840-1926)
Private Collection/ Photo © Lefevre Fine Art Ltd., London/ The Bridgeman Art Library
Nationality / copyright status: French / out of copyright
Adaptation by Jen McClellan

ISBN 978-1-4950-1315-7

HAL•LEONARD®
CORPORATION
7777 W. BLUEMOUND RD. P.O. BOX 13819 MILWAUKEE, WI 53213

In Australia Contact:
Hal Leonard Australia Pty. Ltd.
4 Lentara Court
Cheltenham, Victoria, 3192 Australia
Email: ausadmin@halleonard.com.au

Visit Hal Leonard Online at
www.halleonard.com

JOURNEY THROUGH THE CLASSICS:
Book 3 Reference Chart

✔ WHEN COMPLETED	PAGE	TITLE	COMPOSER	ERA	KEY	METER	CHALLENGE ELEMENTS
	5	Etude	Czerny	Classical	C	$\frac{4}{4}$	Both hands in 𝄞; repeated notes in LH; legato harmonic intervals
	6	Arabesque	Burgmüller	Romantic	Am	$\frac{2}{4}$	16th notes; RH and LH shifts; legato/staccato coordination
	8	Humming Song	Schumann	Romantic	C	$\frac{3}{4}$	Both hands in 𝄞; legato touch; balance and melody/accompaniment in one hand
	10	Russian Folk Song	Beethoven	Classical	Am	$\frac{2}{4}$	Vertical reading; shifting chords
	11	The Bear	Rebikoff	Romantic	C	$\frac{2}{4}$	Both hands in 𝄢; broken LH octaves; reading accidentals
	12	Musette	Bach (notebook)	Baroque	D	$\frac{2}{4}$	D major key signature; 16th notes; quick hand shifts; legato/staccato coordination
	14	Sonatina in G	Attwood	Classical	G	$\frac{4}{4}$	Alberti bass; legato/staccato coordination; articulation and phrasing
	16	Ecossaise	Beethoven	Classical	G	$\frac{2}{4}$	Broken LH octave shifts; 16th notes; syncopation; D.C. al Fine
	17	Tarantella	Spindler	Romantic	C	$\frac{3}{8}$	$\frac{3}{8}$ time signature; very fast scale passages; legato/staccato coordination
	20	Russian Polka	Glinka	Romantic	Dm	$\frac{2}{4}$	16th notes; frequent LH shifts; accents; legato/staccato coordination
	21	Spanish Dance	Oesten	Romantic	Am	$\frac{3}{4}$	16th notes; repeating LH chords; accents; articulation
	22	Sonatina in C	Latour	Classical	C	$\frac{4}{4}$	Continuous scale patterns; LH/RH coordination
	24	Wild Rider	Schumann	Romantic	Am	$\frac{6}{8}$	Fingerings in broken chord patterns; staccato touch; frequent hand shifts
	26	Theme and Variation	Gurlitt	Romantic	G	$\frac{2}{4}$	Connecting pedal; portato touch; phrasing; triplets; balance
	28	Sonatina in C	Clementi	Classical	C	¢	Scale passages; alberti bass; broken arpeggios in both hands; articulation
	30	Minuet and Trio	Mozart, W.A.	Classical	G	$\frac{3}{4}$	Articulation and phrasing; triplets; 16th notes; frequent hand shifts
	32	Menuet in D Minor	Bach (notebook)	Baroque	Dm	$\frac{3}{4}$	Contrapuntal style; frequent hand shifts; leaping intervals; LH/RH coordination
	34	Solfeggio	Bach, J.C.F.	Baroque	D	¢	Continuous 16th note passages; fingerings in broken chord patterns
	36	Minuet in G	Bach (notebook)	Baroque	G	$\frac{3}{4}$	Broken chord arpeggios in both hands; triplets; articulation
	38	Tolling Bell	Heller	Romantic	Bm	$\frac{3}{4}$	Pedal technique; broken chord patterns in both hands; choreography of both hands
	40	Bourrée in E Minor	Bach, J.S.	Baroque	Em	¢	Articulation and phrasing; LH/RH coordination; frequent hand shifts
	42	The Limpid Stream	Burgmüller	Romantic	G	$\frac{4}{4}$	Balance with melody/accompaniment in one hand; LH melody; triplets
	44	The Murmuring Brook	Gurlitt	Romantic	G	$\frac{2}{4}$	Balance with melody/accompaniment in one hand; LH melody; 16th notes
	46	Quiet Morning	Maykapar	Romantic	F	$\frac{12}{8}$	Pedal technique; $\frac{12}{8}$ time signature; balance and beauty of tone
	47	Waltz	Schubert	Romantic	B♭	$\frac{3}{4}$	Vertical reading, B-flat key signature; balance between hands, articulation

CONTENTS

Etude
Op. 823, No. 2

Carl Czerny
(1791-1857)

Arabesque

Op. 100, No. 2

Friedrich Burgmüller
(1806-1874)

Humming Song
Op. 68, No. 3

Robert Schumann
(1810-1856)

Russian Folk Song
Op. 107, No. 7

Ludwig van Beethoven
(1770-1827)

The Bear

Vladimir Rebikoff
(1866-1920)

Musette

Notebook for Anna Magdalena Bach
18th century

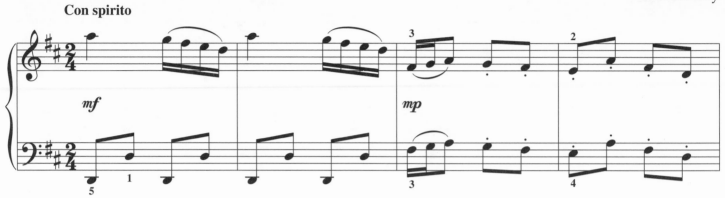

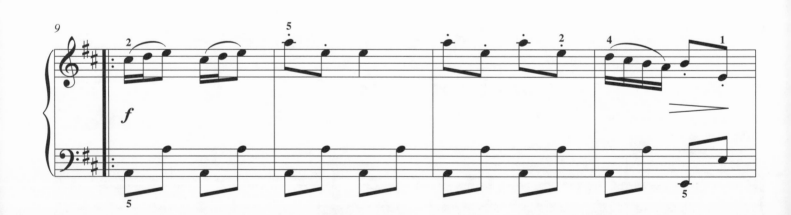

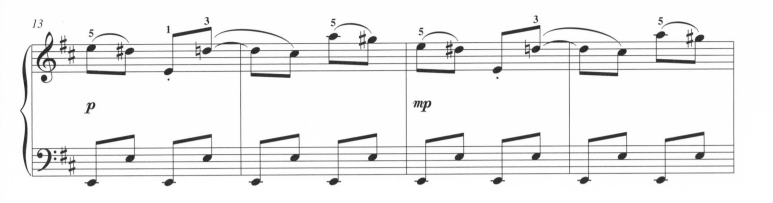

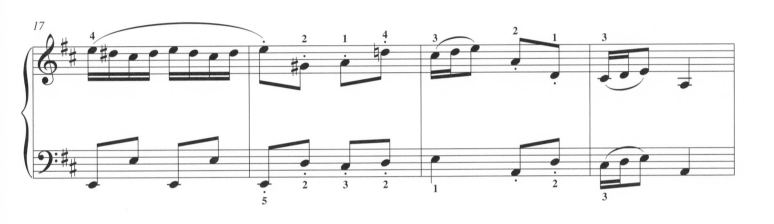

Sonatina in G

Thomas Attwood
(1765-1838)

Ecossaise

Ludwig van Beethoven
(1770-1827)

Tarantella
Op. 157, No. 1

Fritz Spindler
(1817-1905)

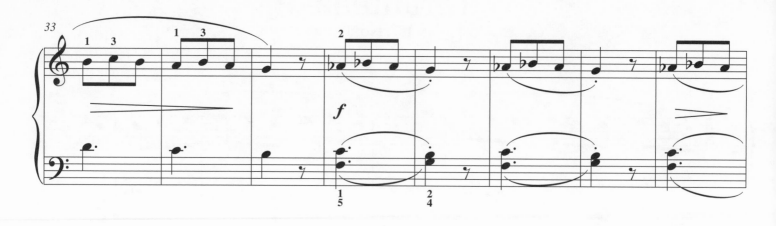

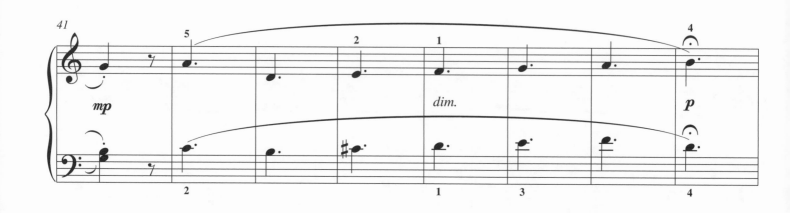

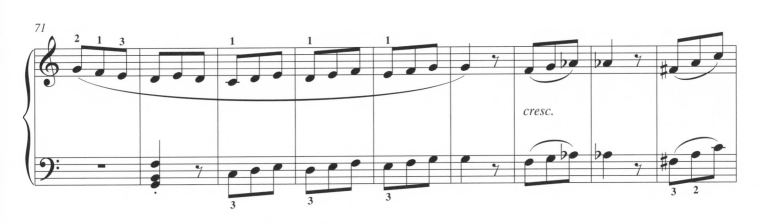

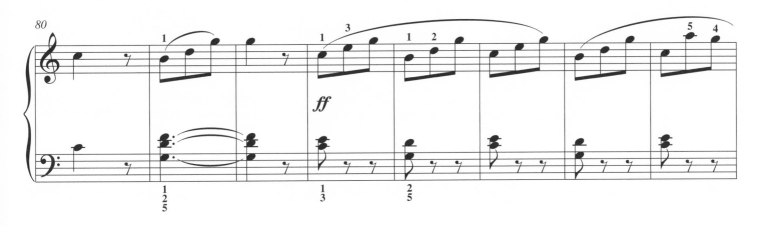

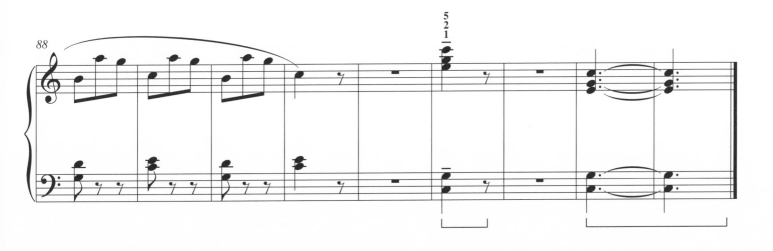

Russian Polka

Michael Ivanovich Glinka
(1804-1857)

Spanish Dance
Op. 61, No. 10

Theodor Oesten
(1813-1870)

Sonatina in C

Jean T. Latour
(1766-1837)

Wild Rider
Op. 68, No. 8

Robert Schumann
(1810-1856)

Theme and Variation
Op. 228

Cornelius Gurlitt
(1820-1901)

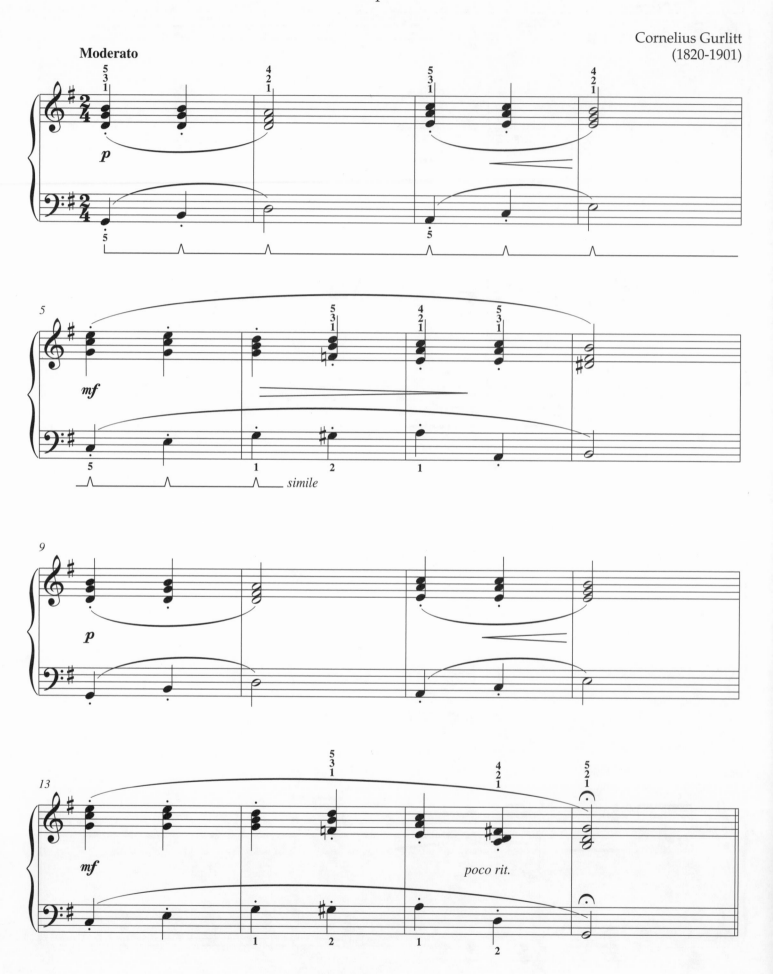

VARIATION

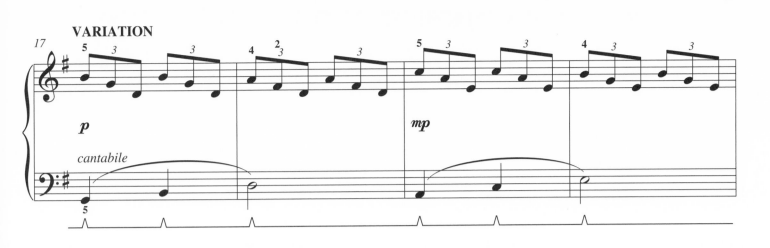

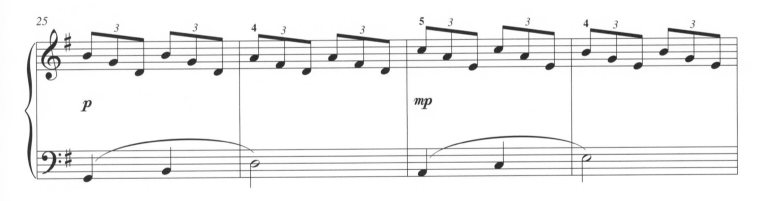

Sonatina in C

I

Muzio Clementi
(1752-1832)

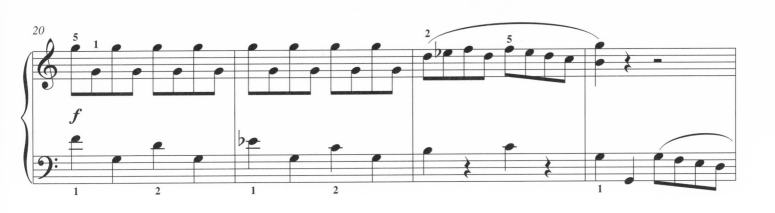

Minuet and Trio

Wolfgang Amadeus Mozart
(1756-1791)

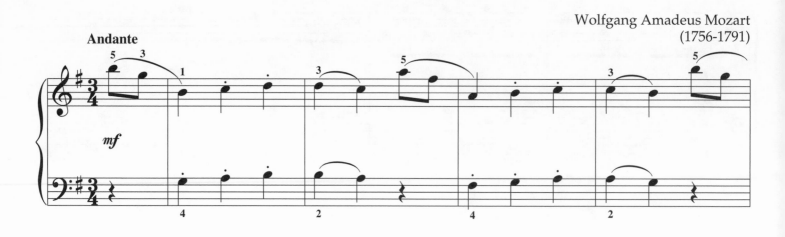

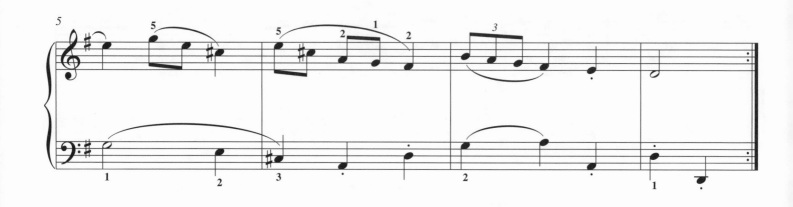

Menuet in D Minor

Notebook for Anna Magdalena Bach
18th century

Solfeggio

Johann Christoph Friedrich Bach
(1732-1795)

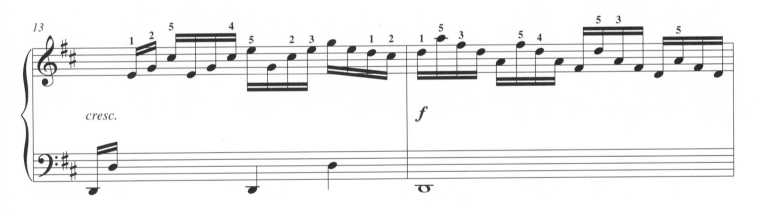

Minuet in G

Notebook for Anna Magdalena Bach
18th century

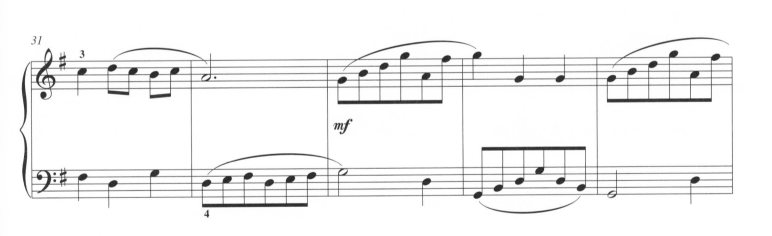

Tolling Bell

Op. 125, No. 8

Stephen Heller
(1813-1888)

Bourrée in E Minor
BWV 996

Johann Sebastian Bach
(1685-1750)

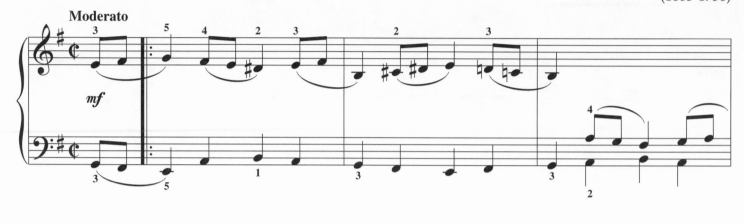

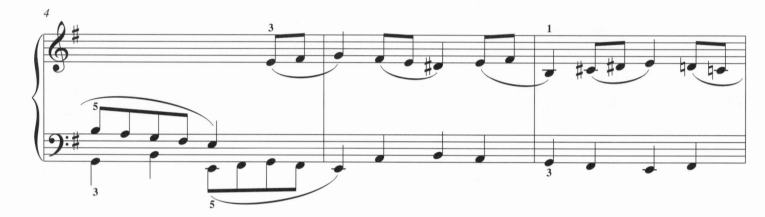

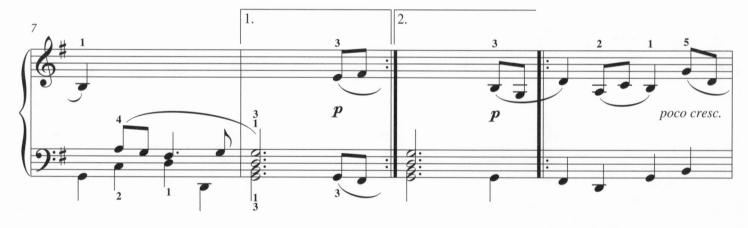

The Limpid Stream
Op. 100, No. 7

Friedrich Burgmüller
(1806-1874)

The Murmuring Brook
Op. 140, No. 5

Cornelius Gurlitt
(1820-1901)

Quiet Morning

Samuel Maykapar
(1867-1938)

Waltz
Op. 127, No. 15

Franz Schubert
(1797-1828)

SCHIRMER
PERFORMANCE EDITIONS
BOOK ONLY EDITIONS

Pedagogical in nature, these editions offer insightful interpretive suggestions, pertinent fingering, and historical and stylistic commentary.

The book with audio versions remain available as well, priced slightly higher. Visit **halleonard.com** to see a listing of all book/audio versions available.

J.S. BACH: FIRST LESSONS IN BACH
ed. Christos Tsitsaros
00297090...$9.99

J.S. BACH: TWO-PART INVENTIONS
ed. Christopher Taylor
00297091...$7.99

J. FRIEDRICH BURGMÜLLER: 25 PROGRESSIVE STUDIES, OP. 100
ed. Margaret Otwell
00297086...7.99

FREDERIC CHOPIN: PRELUDES
ed. Brian Ganz
00297085...$9.99

MUZIO CLEMENTI: SONATINAS, OP. 36
ed. Jennifer Linn
00297087...$7.99

CARL CZERNY: PRACTICAL METHOD FORBEGINNERS, OP. 599
ed. Matthew Edwards
00297083...$9.99

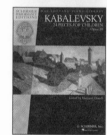

CARL CZERNY: SCHOOL OF VELOCITY, OP. 299
ed. Matthew Edwards
00297084...$8.99

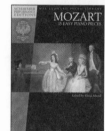

DMITRI KABALEVSKY: 24 PIECES FOR CHILDREN OP. 39
ed. Margaret Otwell
00297092...$10.99

W.A. MOZART: 15 EASY PIANO PIECES
ed. Elena Abend
00297088...$7.99

ERIK SATIE: GYMNOPEDIES AND GNOSSIENNES
ed. Matthew Edwards
00297089...$7.99

THE 20TH CENTURY – ELEMENTARY LEVEL
compiled and edited by Richard Walters
00297094...$9.99

THE 20TH CENTURY – INTERMEDIATE LEVEL
compiled and edited by Richard Walters
00297097...$10.99

G. SCHIRMER, Inc.

For More Information, See Your Local Music Dealer, Or Write To:

HAL•LEONARD® CORPORATION
7777 W. Bluemound Rd. P.O. Box 13819 Milwaukee, WI 53213

Prices, contents and availability subject to change without notice. 0115